LOVE
FOR A *Lifetime*

PRESENTED TO

_____

FROM

_____

DATE

_____

DR. JAMES DOBSON

LOVE
FOR A
Lifetime

*Building a Marriage
That Will Go
the Distance*

This book is dedicated to my wonderful wife, Shirley,

with whom I have lived and loved for more than forty years.

I thank God every day for His gift of this special lady.

LOVE FOR A *Lifetime*

©1987, 1993, 1996, 1998, 2003 by James Dobson, Inc.
published by Multnomah Gifts™,
a division of Multnomah® Publishers, Inc.
P.O. Box 1720, Sisters, Oregon 97759

International Standard Book Number: 1-59052-0874

Design by Koechel Peterson Design, Inc., Minneapolis, Minnesota

Excerpts from: *Straight Talk to Men and Their Wives* by James C. Dobson, ©1980 by Multnomah Publishers; *Love Must Be Tough* by Dr. James C. Dobson, ©1983 by Multnomah Publishers; *Night Light* by James Dobson, Inc., © 2000 by Multnomah Publishers; *What Wives Wish Their Husbands Knew about Women* by Dr. James C. Dobson, ©1975 by Tyndale House Publishers, Inc., Wheaton, Illinois. Used by permission.

Unless otherwise indicated, Scripture quotations are from *The Holy Bible,* King James Version. Other Scripture quotations are from: *The Holy Bible,* New International Version (NIV). © 1973, 1984 by International Bible Society, used by permission of Zondervan Publishing House.

Multnomah is a trademark of Multnomah Publishers, Inc., and is registered in the U.S. Patent and Trademark Office. The colophon is a trademark of Multnomah Publishers, Inc.

Library of Congress Cataloging-in-Publication Data

Dobson, James C., 1936-

　　Love for a Lifetime

Marriage—Religious aspects—Christianity.

　　I. Title.

　　BV835.D63　1987　　248.8'4　　　87-14117

Printed in Belgium

For information:
MULTNOMAH PUBLISHERS, INC.
POST OFFICE BOX 1720
SISTERS, OREGON 97759

04 05 06 07 08 — 10 9 8 7 6 5 4 3 2 1 0

TABLE OF *Contents*

You can build a stable, satisfying,

intimate relationship that will withstand

the storms of life.

❧

NEWLYWED
Games

> Love…always protects,
> always trusts, always hopes,
> always perserveres.
>
> I CORINTHIANS 13:6-7 NIV

OME YEARS AGO, I was flipping through the channels on our television and paused momentarily to watch one of those "newly-wed" game shows. It was a bad decision. The leering host posed a series of dumb questions to a lineup of flaky brides whose equally weird husbands were "sequestered backstage in a soundproof room."

He challenged the women to predict their husband's answers to inquiries that went something like this:

"Where was the exact spot your husband saw you stark naked for the first time?"

"If you and your husband ever separated, which of his friends would be the first to make a pass at you?"

"How would you describe the first time you and your husband 'made whoopee' using these TV terms: First Run, Rerun, or Cancelled?"

Without the least hesitation, the women blurted out frank answers to these and other intimate questions. At times I felt I shouldn't be watching, and indeed, past generations would have blushed and gasped. But the host was undaunted. He then asked the wives, "What kind of insect does your husband remind you of when he's feeling romantic?" If you think the question was ridiculous, consider the answer given by one female contestant. "A bear," she giggled. When her husband realized she couldn't tell an insect from a mammal, he pounded her with his answer card. She said, "Welllll...I didn't know!"

A few minutes later, the men were given an opportunity to humiliate their wives. They grabbed it. Among other questions designed to produce hostility, they were asked to complete this sentence: "You haven't seen ugly until you've seen my wife's _____." What "fun" to watch the brides squirm as their husbands described their anatomical deficiencies to millions of viewers! Throughout the program the men and women continued to club one another on the head with their answer cards and call each other "stupid." That did it. I couldn't watch any more.

It has been said that television programming reflects the values of the society it serves. Heaven help us if that is true. The impulsive responses of the newlyweds revealed their immaturity, selfishness, hostility, vulnerability, and sense of inadequacy. These are the prime ingredients of marital instability, and too commonly,

By intimacy, I'm referring to the mystical bond of friendship, understanding, and commitment that almost defies explanation.

divorce itself. An army of disillusioned ex-husbands and ex-wives can attest to that all too well.

For every ten new marriages in America today, five will end in bitter conflict and divorce. That is tragic, but have you ever wondered what happens to the other five? Do they sail blissfully into the sunset? Hardly! According to clinical psychologist Neil Warren, all five will stay together for a lifetime, but in varying degrees of disharmony. On a *Focus on the Family* radio broadcast, Dr. Warren quoted the research of Dr. John Cuber, whose findings were published in a book entitled *The Significant Americans*. Cuber learned that some couples will remain married for the benefit of the children, while others will pass the years in relative apathy. Incredibly, only one or two couples in ten will achieve what might be called "intimacy" in their marriages.

By *intimacy*, Dr. Cuber was referring to the mystical bond of friendship, understanding, and commitment that almost defies explanation. It occurs when a man and woman, starting out as separate and distinct individuals, fuse into a single unit, which the Bible calls "one flesh." I'm convinced that the human spirit craves this kind of unconditional love and that women, especially, experience something akin to "soul hunger" when it cannot be achieved. I'm also certain that most couples expect to find intimacy in marriage, yet somehow it often eludes them.

Fortunately, you and your partner are not merely passive victims in the unfolding drama of your lives together. You *can* build a stable, satisfying, intimate relationship that will withstand the storms of life. All you need is a little wise counsel...and a burning desire to succeed.

A man will leave his father and mother
and be united to his wife,
and they will become one flesh.

GENESIS 2:24

Love for a Lifetime is designed to help you do just that. It is intended especially for single adults, engaged couples, and husbands and wives who have not yet celebrated their tenth anniversaries. This book offers principles and concepts that can armor-plate a marriage and equip it to go the distance. Some of these ideas were gleaned directly from a panel of husbands and wives who have enjoyed successful marriages for thirty, forty, or fifty years. Other material is based on the research of respected experts in the field. We will also examine the major pitfalls that can waylay a relationship and offer advice on how to avoid them. Ultimately, of course, we will rely on the principles endorsed by the Creator of families Himself. That is pretty safe counsel, to be sure.

So let's get started! There is no better time than these early years to lay the proper foundation for a rock-solid marriage. To begin, I hope you'll forget everything you've seen on those newlywed game shows. Unless, perhaps, you'd like to tell us about the last time you would have, if you could have, beat your spouse on the head with a frying pan. Move over, game show hosts. I can ask dumb questions, too! ❧

What greater thing is there

for two human souls

than to feel that they are joined...

to strengthen each other...

to be at one with each other

in silent, unspeakable memories.

GEORGE ELIOT

The key to a healthy marriage

is to keep your eyes wide open

before you wed...

and half closed thereafter.

EYES
Wide Open

> Matrimony...
> offers the most fulfilling
> human relationship
> possible.

A YOUNG MAN FELL IN LOVE with a pretty young lady. He took her home to meet his mother before asking her to marry him. But his mother disliked the girl intensely and refused to give her blessing. Three times this happened with different marriage candidates, leaving the young man exasperated. Finally, in desperation, he found a girl who was amazingly like his mother. They walked, talked, and even looked alike. *Surely my mother will approve of this selection,* he thought. With great anticipation he took his new friend home to be considered...and behold, his *father* hated her!

This young man had a problem, but his predicament was hardly unique. Finding the right person to love for a lifetime can be one of the greatest challenges in living. By the time you locate a sane, loyal, mature, disciplined, intelligent, motivated, chaste, kind, unselfish, attractive, and godly partner, you're too worn out to care. Furthermore, merely *locating* Mr. or Miss Marvelous is only half the assignment; getting that person interested in you is another matter.

And it's not becoming any easier to find and keep the right partner. At this writing, 1.1 million divorces occur in the United States every year.[1] The average duration of first marriages that end in divorce is only eight years.[2] What a tragedy! Not one of these couples anticipated the conflict and pain that quickly settled into their marriage. They were shocked...surprised...dismayed. When they stood at the altar and promised to be faithful forever, they never dreamed they were making the greatest mistake of their lives.

Part of the problem is that many men and women enter marriage having had no healthy role models in their formative years. If nearly half of all families are splitting up today, that means that almost half of all marriageable young adults have seen only conflict and disillusionment at home. It's no wonder that these newlyweds often sputter and fumble their way through early married life.

Some choose not to marry at all because of their skepticism about long-term relationships. Consider the words of a popular song from an earlier era, by Carly

Simon and Jacob Brackman. The lyrics are devastating. In effect, they say it's impossible to achieve intimacy in marriage; such a life will be lonely, meaningless, and sterile.

> *My friends from college they're all married now:*
>
> *They have their houses and their lawns.*
>
> *They have their silent noons.*
>
> *Tearful nights, angry dawns.*
>
> *Their children hate them for the things they're not:*
>
> *They hate themselves for what they are.*
>
> *And yet they drink, they laugh.*
>
> *Close the wound, hide the scar.*
>
> *But you say it's time we moved in together*
>
> *And raise a family of our own, you and me.*
>
> *Well, that's the way I've always heard it should be:*
>
> *You want to marry, we'll marry.*[3]

How strongly I disagree with the message in this sad song! After more than forty wonderful years of matrimony with Shirley, I can state unequivocally not only that marriage is still workable, but that it offers the most fulfilling human relationship possible. The family was God's idea and He does not make mistakes. He observed the loneliness that plagued Adam in the Garden of Eden and gave him a woman to share his thoughts with and to feel his touch. There is nothing quite like being loved unconditionally and intimately, decade after decade, by someone who promises to be there for better or worse, all the rest of your days.

Indeed, marriage is marvelous when functioning as intended—but therein lies the problem. Many of us fall into certain behavioral patterns that weaken the marital bond and interfere with a long-term relationship.

Among these destructive patterns is the tendency for young men and women to marry virtual strangers. Oh, I know that a typical couple talks for countless hours during the courtship period and believes they know each other. But a dating relationship is designed to *conceal* information. Each partner puts his or her best foot forward, hiding embarrassing facts, habits, and flaws.

Plans fail for lack of counsel, but with many advisers they succeed.

PROVERBS 15:22

There is nothing quite like being loved unconditionally and intimately, decade after decade, by someone who promises to be there for better or worse...

Consequently, the bride and groom who tie the knot too quickly begin marriage with an array of false assumptions about how life will be after the wedding. Major conflicts occur a few weeks later when they discover that they differ radically on what each considers non-negotiable issues. The stage is set for arguments and hurt feelings.

Equally dangerous is the decision to live together before marriage. This is a bad idea for many reasons. First, it leads to sexual immorality that dishonors God (see 1 Corinthians 6:18–20). Second, it undermines the relationship. Studies show that couples who live together before marriage have a greater than 50 percent chance of divorce than those who don't. Researchers found that those who cohabit later regretted having "violated their moral standards" and "felt a loss of personal freedom to exit out the back door." [4]

What, then, is the best approach for couples who feel they are on a path to marriage? I strongly recommend premarital counseling. Each engaged couple, even those who seem perfectly suited to one another, should participate in at least six to ten sessions with someone who is trained to help them prepare for marriage. These encounters should help identify the assumptions each partner holds so the couple can work through areas of potential conflict. The following questions touch on issues that should be discussed in the presence of a counselor or pastor:

- Where will you live?

- Will you both work? For how long?

- What about children? How many? How soon? How far apart?

- Will the wife return to work after babies arrive? How quickly?

- How will the kids be disciplined? Fed? Trained?

- What church will you attend?

- What theological differences need to be reckoned with?

- How will your roles vary?

- How will you respond to your in-laws?

- Where will you spend Thanksgiving and Christmas?

- How will financial decisions be made? Who will write the checks?

- How do each of you feel about credit?

- Will you buy a car on credit? How soon? What kind?

- How far do you expect to go sexually before marriage?

- If the bride's friends differ from the groom's, how will you relate to them?

- What are your greatest apprehensions about your fiancé(e)?

- What other expectations do you have?

As couples go through these questions, surprises often turn up. Some prospective husbands and wives discover major problems and agree to postpone or call off the wedding. Others work through their conflicts and proceed with increased confidence. All benefit from getting to know each other better.

Someone has said: The key to a healthy marriage is to keep your eyes wide open before you wed and half closed thereafter. I agree.

Noted counselor and author Norman Wright discussed his views on premarital counseling during a *Focus on the Family* radio broadcast some years ago and made several significant observations:

1. Couples should not announce their engagement or select a wedding date until at least half of the counseling sessions are completed. That way they can gracefully go their separate ways if unresolvable problems emerge.

2. Couples need to think through the implications of their decisions regarding children. For example, when an engaged man and woman indicate that they intend to have three children, each three years apart, it means they will not be alone at home for twenty-six more years once the first child is born! Couples are often stunned at hearing this. They should talk about how they will nurture their relationship and keep it alive throughout the parenting years.

3. Spiritual incompatibility is common among couples today. A man and woman may share the same belief system, but often one partner is relatively less mature than the other. One approach is for couples to pray together silently for three to four minutes a day, and then share their prayers out loud. After they are married, Wright recommends they ask one another each morning, "How can I pray for you today?" Then at the end of the day they can ask again about the issues raised in the morning and pray about them together. That's a fine way to handle stress in any relationship!

4. Another frequent source of conflict is parental dependence by one or both partners. This problem is more likely to occur if an individual has never lived away from home. To overcome this difficulty, additional measures must be taken to lessen the dependency. Parental overprotection and interference can be a marriage killer if not recognized and handled properly.

5. Many loving parents today pay for premarital counseling as a gift. I think this is an excellent idea and may be the greatest contribution mothers and fathers will ever make to long-term marriage in the next generation.

Love does not consist in gazing at each other, but in looking in the same direction.

ANTOINE-deSAINT-EXUPERY

In addition to premarital counseling, another wonderful way to eliminate the unpleasant surprises of early married life is a program offered by many churches called Engaged Encounter. During a weekend retreat, engaged couples learn to communicate and understand each other better. Having participated with Shirley in a Marriage Encounter program based on similar concepts, I can attest to its value. That weekend was a highlight of our lives together. I strongly recommend Engaged Encounter to every couple planning a wedding. For more information, write to:

Engaged Encounter

1509 South Forest Street

Denver, Colorado 80222-3831

303-753-9407

Premarital counseling and Engaged Encounter are two great ways to get a marriage off on the right foot. Without specific effort to overcome the barriers to understanding, the honeymoon could be a blind date with destiny.

There is a better way! ✤

Blessed is the man

who finds wisdom,

the man who gains understanding.

PROVERBS 3:13 NIV

It is our uniqueness

that gives freshness and vitality

to a relationship.

VIVE LA
Différence

_M_Y WIFE, SHIRLEY, AND I HAVE BEEN BLESSED with a wonderful relationship. She is my best friend, and I would rather spend an evening with her than with anyone else on earth. But we are also unique individuals and have struggled at times with our differences.

Our most serious conflict has raged now for forty-plus years, with no solution in sight. The problem is that we operate on entirely different internal heating mechanisms. I am very hot-blooded and prefer a Siberian climate. Shirley has ice in her veins and shivers even in warm surroundings. She has concluded that if we can have only one flesh between us, she's going to make it sweat! She will slip over to the thermostat at home and spin the dial to at least eighty-five degrees. All the bacteria in the house jump for joy and begin reproducing like crazy. Within a few minutes I start to glow and begin throwing open doors and windows. This ridiculous tug-of-war has been going on since our honeymoon and will continue till death do us part. In fact, there have been a few times when I thought death *would* part us over this difficulty!

What is interesting to me is how many other husbands and wives struggle with this problem. It also plagues men and women who fight over the office thermostat. Why is temperature such a pressure point? Because women typically operate at a lower rate of metabolism than men. This is only one of the countless physiological and emotional differences between the sexes that we must understand if we hope to live together in harmony.

Genesis tells us that the Creator made two sexes, not one, and that He designed each gender for a specific purpose. Take a good look at male and female anatomy and it becomes obvious that we were crafted to "fit" together. This is true not only in a sexual context, but psychologically as well. Eve, being suited to Adam's particular needs, was given to him as a "help-meet." Man and woman were each divinely fashioned to complement the other.

Even a cursory examination of our biological differences can give us a greater appreciation for the unique and wonderful way we are made. Here is a quick rundown of a few:

1. Men and women differ in every cell of their bodies. This is because each carries a different chromosome pattern that is the basic source of their maleness or femaleness.

2. Women have greater constitutional vitality, perhaps because of this chromosome difference. Normally, women in the United States out-live men by three or four years.

3. Men have a higher rate of basal metabolism than women.

4. The sexes differ in skeletal structure, woman having a shorter head, broader face, less-protruding chin, shorter legs, and longer trunk. The first finger of a woman's hand is usually longer than the third; with men the reverse is true. Men's teeth typically last longer than do those of women.

5. Women have a larger stomach, kidneys, liver, and appendix and have smaller lungs.

6. Women have three important physiological functions totally absent in men—menstruation, pregnancy, and lactation. Each of these significantly influences behavior and feelings. Female hormonal patterns are more complex and varied than male. The glands work differently in the two sexes. For example, a woman's thyroid is larger and more

active; it enlarges during menstruation and pregnancy, which makes her more prone to goiter, and is associated with the smooth skin, relatively hairless body, and thin layer of subcutaneous fat that are important elements in the concept of personal beauty. Women are also more responsive emotionally, laughing and crying more readily.

7. Women's blood contains more water (20 percent fewer red cells). Since red cells supply oxygen to the body, she tires more easily and is more prone to faint. Her constitutional viability is therefore strictly a long-range matter. When the working day in British factories under wartime conditions was increased from ten to twelve hours, accidents among women increased 150 percent; the rate of accidents among men did not increase significantly.

8. Men are 50 percent stronger than women in brute strength.

9. Women's hearts beat more rapidly (eighty vs. seventy-two beats per minute on average); blood pressure (ten points lower than men) varies from minute to minute; but they have less tendency to high blood pressure—at least when the comparison is to women who have not yet experienced menopause.

Man and woman were each divinely fashioned to complement the other.

10. Female lung capacity is about 30 percent less than
    in males.

11. Women can withstand high temperature better than
    men because their metabolism slows down less.[5]

In addition to these physiological differences, the sexes are blessed with a vast array of unique emotional characteristics. It is a wise and dedicated husband who desires to understand his wife's psychological needs and then sets out to meet them. Is she a morning person? If not, bring her a cup of coffee to help her start the day. Does she want to talk the moment she opens her eyes? It is unlikely—but if she feels that way, set aside a few minutes each morning for casual conversation. An observant man can discover countless ways to serve and warm the heart of his wife.

The emotional differences between you and your partner will influence every aspect of your relationship. Your love life is no exception. Briefly stated, in women, love is linked to self-esteem. For a man, romantic experiences with his wife are warm and enjoyable and memorable—but are not considered necessary. For a woman, they are her lifeblood. Her confidence, her sexual response, and her zest for living are often directly related to those tender moments when she feels deeply loved and appreciated by her man. That is why flowers and candy and cards are more meaningful to her than to him. This is why she is continually trying to pull him away from the television set or the newspaper, and not vice versa. This is why the anniversary is critically important to her and why she never forgets it. That is why he had better *not* forget it!

This need for romantic love is not some quirk or peculiarity of the wife, as some husbands may think. It is the way God designed the human female, and the sooner men understand this, the better they will be equipped to increase the level of intimacy in their marriages.

Men also need to realize that women tend to care more about the home and everything in it. I don't know whether your wife or fiancée has a nesting instinct, but for years I have observed this feminine interest in the details of the family dwelling. Admittedly, not every woman lives in a neat house. I know some messy ladies whose mothers must have been frightened by garbage trucks when they were pregnant! Yet even these women show a genuine concern for their house and what is in it. Husbands sometimes fail to comprehend the significance of this female inclination.

Shirley and I recognized that we had differing perspectives several years ago when we purchased a gas barbecue unit for use in our backyard. We hired a plumber to install the device and left for the day. When we returned, we both noticed that the barbecue was mounted about eight inches too high. Shirley and I stood looking at the appliance and our reactions were quite different.

I said, "Yes, it's true. The plumber made a mistake. The barbecue is a bit too high. By the way, what's for dinner tonight?"

Shirley reacted more emphatically. "I don't think I can stand that thing sticking up in the air like that!"

I could have lived the rest of my life without ever thinking about the barbecue mounting again, but to Shirley it was a big deal. Why? Because we see the home differently. So we called the plumber and had him lower the unit about eight inches.

Husbands aren't the only ones who need to be aware of their partners' needs, of course. I suggest that wives tune in to their husbands' quirks and interests as well. For example, a survey taken several years ago to determine what men care about most yielded surprising results. Men did not long for expensive furniture, well-equipped garages, or a private study. What they wanted most was *tranquillity* at home. Competition in the workplace today is so fierce, and the stresses of pleasing a boss and surviving professionally are so severe, that the home needs to be a haven to which a man can retreat. It is a smart woman who tries to make her home what her husband needs it to be.

Of course, many women also work, and their husbands are not the only ones in need of tranquillity. This is a major problem in two-career families. It is even more difficult in the single-parent situation. I know of no simple solution to those stress points, although I'm convinced that emotional instability and even physical illness can occur in the absence of a "safe place." Creating an environment at home to meet that need should be given priority, regardless of the family structure.

Well, so much for this short discourse on gender distinctiveness. I have attempted to show not only that males and females are different—which any bloke can see—but also that God authored those differences and we should appreciate them. It is our uniqueness that gives freshness and vitality to a relationship. How boring it would be if the sexes were identical! How redundant it would have been for the Creator to put Adam to sleep and then fashion yet another man from his rib!

No, He brought forth a woman and gave her to Adam. He put greater toughness and aggressiveness in the man, and more softness and nurturance in the woman—and suited them to one another's needs. And in their relationship He symbolized the mystical bond between the believer and Christ Himself. What an incredible concept!

I say to you, husbands and wives, celebrate your uniqueness and learn to compromise when male and female individuality collide. Or, as an unnamed Frenchman once said, "Vive la différence!" He must have been a happily married man. ❧

*T*here is no more lovely,

friendly or charming

relationship, communion, or company

than a good marriage.

MARTIN LUTHER

Physical intimacy in marriage

is the ultimate demonstration of profound,

romantic love.

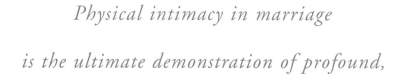

BODY TO BODY,
Soul to Soul

WHEN A HUSBAND AND WIFE achieve true intimacy, they enjoy and appreciate each other at the deepest level. By God's design, one of the most pleasurable ways for couples to express their profound love and appreciation is through His gift of sexual intimacy.

Some would say that "having sex" and "making love" are one and the same, but there's an important distinction between the two. The physical act of intercourse can be accomplished by any appropriately matched members of the animal kingdom. But the art of making love, as intended by God, is a much more meaningful and complex experience. It is physical, emotional, and spiritual.

In marriage we should settle for nothing less than a sexual relationship that is expressed not only body to body, but also heart to heart and soul to soul. This intimate union, two becoming "one flesh" (Genesis 2:24), is both the symbol and fruit of genuine, heartfelt romantic love between a husband and wife.

Of course, married partners often define romantic love in different ways. A woman is inclined to associate romance not just with the bedroom, but with the things a man does throughout the day and week to make her feel loved, protected, and respected. Flowers, compliments, nonsexual touching, and love notes are all steps in this direction. So is helping out at home. A man who shares in the duties of cooking, cleaning, and picking up the kids after basketball practice is much more likely to win the affection of his wife.

Men, on the other hand, rely more on their senses. They appreciate a wife who makes herself as attractive as possible. A man also wants to be respected—and, even better, admired—by his wife. He likes to hear his wife express genuine interest in his opinions, hobbies, and work.

The art of making love…is physical, emotional, and spiritual.

Perhaps the most evocative descriptions of romantic love come from Solomon's Song of Songs, where we see that it includes both

intimacy and emotional excitement: "My lover is mine and I am his" (2:16); "My heart began to pound for him" (5:4). We see how deep affection inspires desire and complete appreciation for another: "How beautiful you are, my darling!" (4:1). We learn that to be romantic means to pursue the object of our affection—and to pine when he or she eludes us: "All night long on my bed I looked for the one my heart loves; I looked for him but did not find him" (3:1). And we see how powerfully a public display of affection communicates romantic love: "He has taken me to a banquet hall, and his banner over me is love" (2:4).

Most important of all, we learn that the epitome of deeply felt romantic love—including sexual intimacy—is expressed within the unbreakable bond of marriage. Song of Songs concludes with this eloquent description of the connection between two married lovers: "Love is as strong as death, its jealousy unyielding as the grave. It burns like a blazing fire, like a mighty flame" (8:6).

This fiery, romantic, sexually intimate love is not achieved overnight. It develops between a man and woman through a process called *marital bonding*. Such bonding refers to the emotional covenant that links a man and woman together for life and makes them intensely valuable to one another. It is the specialness that sets those two lovers apart from every other couple on the face of the earth. It is God's gift of intimate companionship.

But how does this bonding occur, and why is it missing in so many marriages today? According to the research of Dr. Desmond Morris, bonding is most likely to develop among those who have moved systematically and slowly through twelve steps during their courtship and early marriage. The following stages represent the progression of physical intimacy from which a permanent commitment often evolves: (1) Eye to body. (2) Eye to eye. (3) Voice to voice. (4) Hand to hand. (5) Hand to shoulder. (6) Hand to waist. (7) Face to face. (8) Hand to head. (9) Hand to body. (10) Mouth to breast. (11) Touching below the waist. (12) Intercourse.[6] The final four steps of physical contact should be reserved for the marital relationship since they are progressively sexual and intensely personal.

What Morris's research shows is that intimacy must proceed slowly if a male-female relationship is to achieve its full potential. When two people love each other deeply and are committed for life, they have usually developed a great volume of understanding between them that would be considered insignificant to anyone else. They share countless private memories unknown to the rest of the world. This is in large measure where their sense of specialness to one another originates. The critical factor is that they have taken these steps *in sequence.*

When later stages are reached prematurely, such as when couples kiss passionately on the first date or have sexual intercourse before marriage, something precious is lost from the relationship.

To prevent this damaging result, I strongly recommend to my unmarried reader that you STAY OUT OF BED UNLESS YOU GO THERE ALONE! Virginity is not only the best foundation for a healthy marriage; it is also God's perfect will for you (1 Corinthians 6:18; Galatians 5:19–21). It is also the only way to avoid sexually transmitted diseases such as HIV, chlamydia, gonorrhea, syphilis, and genital herpes. More than 15 million Americans are infected with these diseases each year; roughly half of these will stay infected for life.[7] The idea that using a condom allows for "safe" sex is a myth. In fact, two government agencies reported in 2001 that there is no evidence that condoms protect against most sexually transmitted diseases.[8] There is no such thing as safe sex, just as there is no safe sin.

Before we conclude our discussion of bonding, let me emphasize that this concept doesn't apply only to courtship experiences. The most successful marriages are those in which husbands and wives regularly journey through the twelve steps to physical intimacy in their daily lives. Touching and talking and holding hands and gazing into one another's eyes and building memories are as important to partners in their midlife years as to newlyweds in their twenties. Indeed, the best way to invigorate a tired sex life is to walk through the twelve steps regularly and with gusto!

Conversely, when sexual intercourse occurs without the stages of intimacy that should have preceded it, the woman is likely to feel used and abused. If you are already married and now regret that the stages of bonding were taken out of order or that important steps were skipped altogether, it is not too late to work your way through them anew. I know of no better way to draw close to the person you love.

Before we leave this subject, let me offer two more points that may eliminate a great deal of anxiety and conflict in the early days of your marriage.

The epitome of deeply felt romantic love… is expressed within the unbreakable bond of marriage.

First, *don't be surprised if sexual intercourse on the honeymoon is less intense and enjoyable than anticipated.* If you have saved yourself for that first night, your level of expectation may exceed reality by a wide margin. And if you have had intercourse before, disappointment is also possible. Because sexual desire is sometimes greater when it reaches for forbidden fruit, stolen moments in the past may surpass the initial marital experience in pleasure and intensity. Be patient!

Every couple is different, of course, and no generalization applies to everyone. Nevertheless, it is common for sexual problems (or sexual coolness, at least) to occur in early married life. For one thing, the transition from "Thou shalt not" to "Thou shalt, regularly and with great passion" is not so easily made by some people. It takes time for one mindset to give way to another. In addition, sexual intercourse in human beings is a highly complex mental process. The frame of mind, the setting, the sense of security, the aromas, the visualizations, the partner's attitude, and one's own modesty all come into play. That's why you shouldn't be surprised or disappointed if everything fails to "click" on the first night...or even the first month.

Second, *understand that men and women differ significantly in their sexual appetites.* For a typical man, intercourse is much more physiological than it is for a typical woman. This means that he is more easily stimulated visually and typically becomes excited more quickly than she does. Within seconds, the idea of sexual relations can enter his mind, and four or five minutes later the act might be finished and he is asleep again.

A woman doesn't function that way. The way she feels about her husband sexually is a by-product of their romantic relationship at the time. If she feels close to him…loved by him…protected by him…she is more likely to desire him physically. Merely seeing his body does not do that much for her. Yes, she is interested in how he looks, but the surge of passion comes not from a stolen glance but from the quality of their interaction. It is born in his touch and his tenderness.

Let me offer seven recommendations that will contribute to lifelong marriage.

1. *Don't rush the courtship period when you feel you have found the "one and only."* Frank Sinatra said it musically, "Take it nice and easy, making all the stops along the way." At least a year is needed to allow the premarital bonding process to occur.

2. *Make the final choice of a marital partner carefully and prayerfully... never impulsively or recklessly.* You are playing for keeps now. Bring to bear every ounce of intelligence and discretion available to you, and then yield the ultimate decision to the will of the Lord. He will guide you if you don't run ahead of Him.

3. *Proceed through the stages of intimacy one at a time and in the order indicated.*

4. *Do not progress to the final stages before marriage: Enter the marriage bed as a virgin.* If it's too late to preserve your virginity, initiate a policy of abstinence today, and don't waver from it until you are wed.

5. *Seek to marry a virgin.* This mutual purity gives special meaning to sex in marriage. No other human being has invaded the secret world that the two of you share because you reserved yourselves exclusively for one another's pleasure and love. That said, there *is* room for forgiveness if your partner has failed in this area in the past.

6. *Remain faithful to your marriage partner for life.* No exceptions!

7. *Continue to meander through the stages of bonding throughout your married life, enjoying the wonder of intimate, romantic love.*

The Lord established the institution of marriage and gave us the gift of physical intimacy as a means of expressing love between husband and wife. As designed by Him, the sexual relationship in marriage is much more than an afterthought or a method to guarantee procreation. When characterized by mutual respect, tenderness, and affection, it is the ultimate demonstration of profound, romantic love between a man and woman. It is also a glue that helps hold marriages together. That's why I wholeheartedly urge you as husband and wife to enjoy "making love" for a lifetime, and investing the effort to give it priority in your lives together.

A personal relationship with

Jesus Christ is the cornerstone of marriage,

giving meaning and purpose

to every dimension of living.

FUNDAMENTALS
of a
Christian Marriage

*I*N AN EFFORT TO DRAW on the experiences of those who have successfully lived together as husbands and wives, some years ago we asked married couples to participate in an informal study. More than six hundred people agreed to speak candidly to the younger generation about the concepts and methods that have worked in their homes. They each wrote comments and recommendations, which were carefully analyzed and compared. The advice they offered is not new, but it certainly represents a great place to begin. In attempting to learn any task, one should start with the *fundamentals*—those initial steps from which everything else will later develop. In this spirit, our panel of six hundred offered three tried-and-tested, back-to-basics recommendations with which no committed Christian would likely disagree.

A Christ-Centered Home

The panel first suggested that newlyweds should establish and maintain a *Christ-centered home.* Everything rests on that foundation. If a young husband and wife are deeply committed to Jesus Christ, they enjoy enormous advantages over a family with no spiritual dimension.

A meaningful prayer life is essential in maintaining a Christ-centered home. Of course, some people use prayer the way they follow their horoscopes, attempting to manipulate an unidentified "higher power." One of my friends teasingly admits that he utters a prayer each morning on the way to work when he passes the doughnut shop. He knows it is unhealthy to eat the greasy pastries, but he loves them dearly. Therefore, he asks the Lord for permission to indulge himself each day.

He'll say, "If it is Your will that I have a doughnut this morning, let there be a parking space available as I circle the block." If no spot can be found for his car, he circles the block and prays again.

Shirley and I have taken our prayer life a bit more seriously. In fact, this communication between man, woman, and God has been *the* stabilizing factor throughout our forty-plus years of married life. In good times, in hard times, in moments of anxiety, and in periods of praise, we have shared this wonderful privilege of talking directly to our heavenly Father. What a concept. No appointment is needed to enter into His presence. We don't have to go through His subordinates or bribe His secretaries. He is simply there, whenever we bow before Him. Some of the highlights of my life have occurred in these quiet sessions with the Lord.

At one point, shortly after Danae earned her driver's license, Shirley and I covenanted between us to pray for our son and daughter at the close of each day. Not only were we concerned about the risk of an automobile accident, but we were also aware of so many other dangers that lurk out there in a city like Los Angeles, where we lived at the time. That part of the world is known for its weirdos, ding-a-lings, and fruitcakes. That's one reason we found ourselves on our knees each evening, asking for divine protection for the teenagers we loved so much.

One night we were particularly tired and collapsed into bed without our benedictory prayer. We were almost asleep before Shirley's voice pierced the night. "Jim," she said. "We haven't prayed for our kids yet today. Don't you think we should talk to the Lord?"

I admit it was very difficult for me to pull my six-foot two-inch frame out of the warm bed that night. Nevertheless, we got on our knees and offered a prayer for our children's safety, placing them in the hands of the Father once more.

Later we learned that Danae and a girlfriend had gone to a fast-food establishment and bought hamburgers and Cokes. They had driven up the road a few miles and were sitting in the car eating the meal when a city police-man drove by, shining his spotlight in all directions. He was obviously looking for someone, but gradually went past.

A few minutes later, Danae and her friend heard a *clunk* from under the car. They looked at one another nervously and felt a sharp bump. Before they could leave, a man crawled out from under the car and emerged on the passenger side. He was very hairy and looked like he had been on the street for weeks. The man immediately came to the door and attempted to open it. Thank God, it was locked. Danae quickly started the car and drove off… no doubt at record speed.

When we checked the timing of this incident, we realized that Shirley and I had been on our knees at the precise moment of danger. Our prayers were answered. Our daughter and her friend were safe!

It is impossible for me to overstate the need for prayer in the fabric of family life. Not simply as a shield against danger, of course. A personal relationship with Jesus Christ is the cornerstone of marriage, giving meaning and purpose to every dimension of living. Being able to bow in prayer as the day begins or ends gives

It is impossible for me to overstate the need for prayer in the fabric of family life.

expression to frustrations and concerns, which might not otherwise be ventilated. On the other end of that prayer line is a loving heavenly Father who has promised to hear and answer our petitions. In this day, when families are disintegrating on every side, we dare not try to make it on our own.

Couples who have not found a common faith are often left in a vulnerable position. One such lady wrote the following letter to me after her husband had left her:

Dear Dr. Dobson:

My husband recently left me after fifteen years of marriage. We had a great physical, emotional, and intellectual relationship. But something was missing…we had no spiritual bond between us.

Please tell young couples that there will always be a void in their lives together without Christ. A good marriage must have its foundation in Him in order to experience lasting love, peace, and joy.

Since my husband walked out on me, I have tried to rebuild my relationship with God. I am now growing steadily in my walk with the Lord, but I am alone.

There is a great truth in this sad letter. The couple that depends on Scripture for solutions to the stresses of living has a distinct advantage over the family with no faith. The Bible they love is the world's most incredible text. It was written by thirty-nine authors who spoke three separate languages and lived in a time frame spanning fifteen hundred years. How miraculous is the work of those inspired writers! If two or three individuals today were to witness a bank robbery, they would probably give conflicting accounts of the incident. Human perception is simply that flawed. Yet those thirty-nine contributors to Scripture, most of whom never even met each other, prepared sixty-six separate books that fit together with perfect continuity and symmetry. The entire Old Testament makes a single statement: "Jesus is coming." And the New Testament declares: "Jesus is here!"

By reading these Holy Scriptures, we are given a window into the mind of the Father. What an incredible resource! The Creator, who began with nothingness and made beautiful mountains and streams and clouds and cuddly little babies, has elected to give us the inside story of the family. Marriage and parenthood were His ideas, and He tells us in His Word how to live together in peace and harmony. Everything from handling money to sexual attitudes is discussed in Scripture, with each prescription bearing the personal endorsement of the King of the universe. Why would anyone disregard this ultimate resource?

Finally, the Christian way of life lends stability to marriage because its principles and values naturally produce harmony. When put into action, Christian teaching emphasizes giving to others, self-discipline, obedience to divine commandments, conformity to the laws of man, and love and fidelity between husband and wife. It is a shield against addictions to alcohol, pornography, gambling, materialism, and other behaviors that could be damaging to the relationship. Is it any wonder that a Christ-centered relationship is the best ground floor for a marriage?

Aleksandr Solzhenitsyn, that great Soviet dissident, once wrote, "If I were called upon to identify briefly the principal trait of the entire twentieth century, here too I would be unable to find anything more precise and pithy than to repeat once again: Men have forgotten God."

Don't let this happen in your home. You probably knelt together and sent a prayer to the Lord during your wedding ceremony. Return to that source daily for strength and stability.

Committed Love

The second suggestion made by our panel of six hundred "experts" represented yet another back-to-basics concept. It focused on *committed love* that is braced against the inevitable storms of life. Very few certainties touch us all in this mortal existence, but one absolute is that we will experience hardship and stress at some point. Nobody remains unscathed. Life will test each of us severely, if not during younger days, then through the events surrounding our final days. Jesus spoke of this inevitability when He said to His disciples, "In the world ye shall have tribulation: but be of good cheer; I have overcome the world" (John 16:33).

Dr. Richard Selzer is a surgeon who has written several outstanding books about his beloved patients, including *Mortal Lessons* and *Letters to a Young Doctor*. In the first of these texts he describes the experience of "horror" that invades one's life sooner or later. When we're young, he says, we seem to be shielded from it the way the body is protected against bacterial infection. Microscopic organisms are all around us, yet our bodies' defenses effectually hold them at bay…at least for a season. Likewise, each day we walk in and through a world of horror unscathed, as though surrounded by an impenetrable membrane of protection.

We may even be unaware that distressing possibilities exist during the period of youthful good health. But then one day, without warning, the membrane tears, and horror seeps into our lives. Until that moment, it was always someone else's misfortune…another man's tragedy…and not our own. The tearing of the membrane can be devastating, especially for those who do not know the "good cheer" (John 16:33) Jesus gives in times of tribulation.

Having served on a large medical school faculty for fourteen years, I have watched husbands and wives in the hours when horror began to penetrate the protective membrane. All too commonly, their marital relationships were shattered by the new stresses that invaded their lives. Parents of a mentally retarded child, for example, often blamed one another for the tragedy that confronted them. Instead of clinging to each other in love and reassurance, they added to their sorrows by attacking their partners. I do not condemn them for this human failing, but I do pity them for it. A basic ingredient was missing in their relationship, which remained unrecognized until the membrane tore. That essential component is called *commitment.*

A number of years ago, I heard the late Dr. Francis Schaeffer speak to this issue.

He described the bridges in Europe built by the Romans in the first and second centuries A.D. They are still standing today, despite the unreinforced brick and mortar with which they were made. Why haven't they collapsed in this modern era of heavy trucks and equipment? The reason they remain intact is because they are used for nothing but foot traffic. If an eighteen-wheel semi were driven across the historic structures, they would crumble in a great cloud of dust and debris.

Committed love is so critical to the success of a marriage.

Marriages that lack an iron-willed determination to hang together at all costs are like those fragile Roman bridges. They appear to be secure and may indeed remain upright—until they are put under heavy pressure. That's when the seams split and the foundation crumbles. It appears to me that the majority of young couples today, like some of those competing on those newlywed game shows, are in that incredibly vulnerable position. Their relationships are constructed of unreinforced mud which will not withstand the weighty trials lying ahead. The determination to survive together simply is not there.

This is why committed love is so critical to the success of a marriage. In stressing the importance of commitment, however, our panel of six hundred was referring not only to the great tragedies of life but also to the daily frustrations that wear and tear on a relationship. These minor irritants, when accumulated over time, may be even more threatening to a relationship than catastrophic events. And yes, Virginia, there are times in every good marriage when a husband and wife don't like each other very much. There are occasions when they feel as though they will never love their partner again. Emotions are like that. They flatten out occasionally, like an automobile tire with a nail in the tread. Riding on the rim is a pretty bumpy experience for everyone on board.

What will you do, then, when unexpected tornadoes blow through your home, or when the doldrums leave your sails sagging and silent? Will you pack it in? Will you pout and cry and seek ways to strike back? Or will your commitment hold you steady? These questions must be addressed *now,* before Satan has an opportunity to put his noose of discouragement around your neck. Set your jaw and clench your fists. Nothing short of death must ever be permitted to come between the two of you. *Nothing!*

This determined attitude is missing from so many marital relationships today. I read of a wedding ceremony in New York years ago in which the bride and groom each pledged "to stay with you for as long as I shall love you." I doubt their marriage lasted even a few years. The *feeling* of love is simply too ephemeral to hold a relationship together for very long. It comes and goes. That's why our panel of six hundred was adamant on this point. They have lived long enough to know that a weak marital commitment will inevitably lead to divorce. One participant wrote:

> *Marriage is no fairy-tale land of enchantment. But you can create an oasis of love in the midst of a harsh world by grinding it out and sticking in there.*

Another said:

> *Perfection doesn't exist. You have to approach the first few years of marriage with a learner's permit to work out your incompatibilities. It is a continual effort.*

Those views don't sound particularly romantic, do they? But they do carry the wisdom of experience. Two people are not compatible simply because they love each other and are both professing Christians. Many young people assume that the sunshine and flowers that characterized their courtship will continue for the rest of their lives. Don't you believe it! It is naïve to expect two unique and strong-willed individuals to fit together easily like a couple of machines. Even gears have multiple cogs with rough edges that must be honed before they will work in concert.

That honing process usually occurs in the first years of marriage. What often happens at this time is a dramatic struggle for power in the relationship. Who will lead? Who will follow? Who will determine how the money is spent? Who will get his way or her way in times of disagreement? Everything is up for grabs in the beginning, and the way these early decisions are made will set the stage for the future.

Therein lays the danger. Abraham Lincoln said, quoting the Lord Jesus, "A house divided against itself cannot stand." If both partners come into the relationship prepared for battle, the foundation will begin to crumble. The apostle Paul gave us the divine perspective on human relationships—not only in marriage but in every dimension of life. He wrote, "Do nothing out of selfish ambition or vain conceit, but in humility consider others better than yourselves" (Philippians 2:3, NIV).

That one verse contains more wisdom than most marriage manuals combined. If heeded, it could virtually eliminate divorce from the catalog of human experience.

Communication

The third recommendation by our panel of six hundred represents another basic ingredient of good marriages. Like the other two, it begins with the letter *c*—good *communication* between husbands and wives. This topic has been beaten to death by writers of marriage books, but I would like to offer some less-overworked thoughts on marital communication that might be useful to young married couples.

First, it must be understood that males and females differ in yet another way not mentioned earlier. Research makes it clear that most little girls are blessed with greater linguistic ability than most little boys, and it remains a lifelong talent. Simply stated, she talks more than he does. As an adult, she typically expresses her feelings and thoughts far better than her husband and is often irritated by his reticence. God may have given her 50,000 words per day and her husband only 25,000. He comes home from work with 24,975

In humility consider others better than yourselves.

PHILIPPIANS 2:3

used up and merely grunts his way through the evening. He may descend into Monday night football, while his wife is dying to expend her remaining 25,000 words. A female columnist commenting on this male tendency even proposed that an ordinance be passed stating that a man who watches 168,000 football games in a single season be declared legally dead. (All in favor say "Aye.")

The complexity of the human personality guarantees exceptions to every generalization. Yet any knowledgeable marriage counselor knows that the inability or unwillingness of husbands to reveal their feelings to their wives is one of the common complaints of women. It can almost be stated as an absolute: Show me a quiet, reserved husband, and I'll show you a frustrated wife. She wants to know what he's thinking, what happened at the office or jobsite, how he views the children, and especially, how he feels about her. The husband, by contrast, finds some things better left unsaid. It is a classic struggle.

The paradox is that a highly emotional, verbal woman is sometimes drawn to the strong, silent type. He seemed so secure and "in control" before they were married. She admired his unflappable nature and his coolness in a crisis. Then they were married, and the

She wants to know what he's thinking… especially, how he feels about her.

flip side of his great strength became obvious. He wouldn't talk! So for the next forty years, she gnashed her teeth because her husband couldn't give what she needed from him. It just wasn't in him.

What is the solution to such communication problems? As always, it involves compromise. A man has a clear responsibility to "cheer up his wife which he hath taken" (Deuteronomy 24:5). He must not claim himself a "rock" who will never allow himself to be vulnerable again. He must press himself to open his heart and share his deeper feelings with his wife. Time must be reserved for meaningful conversations. Taking walks, going out to breakfast, or riding bicycles on a Saturday morning are fresh opportunities for conversation that can help keep love alive. Communication can occur even in families where the husband leans inward and the wife leans outward. In these instances, I believe that the primary responsibility for compromise lies with the husband.

Some women, however, are married to men who will never be able to fully express themselves or understand the feminine needs I have described. Their emotional structure makes it impossible for them to comprehend the feelings and frustrations of another—particularly those occurring in the opposite sex. These men will not read a book such as this and would probably resent it if they did. They have never been required to "give" and have no idea how it is done. What, then, is to be the reaction of their wives? What would you do if your husband lacked the insight to be what you need him to be?

My advice is that you change that which can be altered, explain that which can be understood, teach that which can be learned, revise that which can be improved, resolve that which can be settled, and negotiate that which is open to compromise. Create the best marriage possible from the raw materials brought by two imperfect human beings with two distinctly unique personalities. But for all the rough edges that can never be smoothed and the faults that can never be eradicated, try to develop the best possible perspective and determine in your mind to accept reality exactly as it is. The first principle of mental health is to accept that which cannot be changed. You could easily go to pieces over adverse circumstances that are beyond your control. You can will to hang tough, or you can yield to cowardice. Depression is often evidence of emotional surrender.

Someone wrote:

> *Life can't give me joy and peace,*
> *it's up to me to will it.*
> *Life just gives me time and space,*
> *it's up to me to fill it.*

Can you accept the fact that your husband will never be able to meet all your needs and aspirations? Seldom does one human being satisfy every longing and hope in another. Obviously, this coin has two sides: You can't be his perfect woman either. He is no more equipped to resolve your entire package of emotional needs than you are to become his sexual dream machine every twenty-four hours. Both partners have to settle for human foibles and faults and irritability and fatigue and occasional nighttime "headaches." A good marriage is not one in which perfection reigns; it is a relationship in which a healthy perspective overlooks a multitude of unresolvables. Thank goodness my wife, Shirley, has adopted this attitude toward me!

I am especially concerned about the mother of small children who chooses to stay at home as a full-time homemaker. If she looks to her husband as the provider of all adult conversation and the satisfier of every emotional need, their marriage could quickly run aground. He returns home from work at night somewhat depleted and in need of tranquillity, as we discussed earlier. Instead of tranquillity, he finds a woman who is continually starved for attention and support. When she sees in his eyes that he has nothing left to

A happy marriage is the union of two good forgivers.
ROBERT QUILLEN

give, she becomes either depressed or angry (or both), and he has no idea how he can help her.

I understand this feminine need and have attempted to articulate it to men. Nevertheless, a woman's total dependence on a man places too much pressure on the marital relationship. It sometimes cracks under the strain. What can be done, then? A woman with a normal range of emotional needs cannot simply ignore her needs—they scream for fulfillment.

I have long recommended that women in this situation seek to supplement what their husbands can give by cultivating meaningful female relationships. Having girlfriends with whom they can talk heart to heart, study the Scriptures, and share childcare techniques can be vital to mental health. Without this additional support, loneliness and low self-esteem can build and begin to choke the marriage to death.

Sadly, this is not always easy to implement. In recent years we've witnessed a breakdown in relationships between women. A hundred years ago, wives and mothers did not have to seek female friendship. It was programmed into the culture. Women canned food together, washed clothes at the creek together, and cooperated in church charity work together. When babies were born, the new mother was visited by aunts, sisters, neighbors, and churchwomen who came to help her diaper, feed, and care for the child. An automatic support system surrounded women and made life easier. Its absence translates quickly into marital conflict and can lead to divorce.

To the young wives who are reading these words, *I urge you not to let this happen to you.* Invest time in your female friends—even though you are busy. Resist the temptation to pull into the walls of your home and wait for your husband to be all things to you. Stay involved as a family in a church that meets your needs and preaches the Word. Remember that you are surrounded by many other women with similar feelings. Find them. Care for them. Give to them. And in the process, your own self-esteem will rise. Then when you are content, your marriage will flourish. It sounds simplistic, but that is the way we were designed by an infinitely wise and loving God.

You cannot serve

both God and Money.

MATTHEW 6:24 [NIV]

MONEY:
The Great Mischief-Maker

FIND IT INTERESTING that Jesus spoke more about money than about any other subject. Not only did He talk repeatedly about money, but most of His pronouncements included warnings about it. He had a dramatic encounter with a rich young ruler. He told disturbing parables about Lazarus and the rich young ruler, and about the rich fool. He said, "For where your treasure is, there will your heart be also" (Matthew 6:21), and, "Man shall not live by bread alone, but by every word that proceedeth out of the mouth of God" (Matthew 4:4). And finally, He asked a question that has echoed down through the corridors of time: "For what is a man profited, if he shall gain the whole world, and lose his own soul?" (Matthew 16:26).

Twenty centuries later, we still have to deal with that eternal question.

The intervening years have made it clear why Jesus gave such emphasis to the dangers of money. Men have lusted for it, killed for it, died for it, and gone to hell for it. Money has come between the best of friends and brought down the proud and the mighty. And alas, it has torn millions of marriages limb from limb! Materialism and debt have devastated more families than perhaps any other factor, and believe me, it could destroy your marriage as well.

Men and women tend to have different value systems, which can easily lead to arguments about money. My father, for example, was a hunter, who thought nothing of using three boxes of shotgun shells in an afternoon of recreational shooting. Yet, if my mother spent an equal amount of money on a "useless" potato peeler, he considered it wasteful. Never mind that she enjoyed shopping as much as he did hunting. They simply saw things differently. On a larger scale, this divergence can produce catastrophic arguments over how to allocate limited resources.

Curiously, those with unlimited financial resources are in no less jeopardy. One of the richest men of his time, J. Paul Getty's

Whatever our financial status, there are monetary principles we should understand and apply if we are to protect our families.

estate exceeded $4 billion in net worth. This is what he wrote in his auto-biography:

> I have never been given to envy…save for the envy I feel toward those people who have the ability to make a marriage work and endure happily. It's an art I have never been able to master. My record: five marriages, five divorces. In short, five failures.[9]

Not many of us will have to worry about managing an estate the size of Getty's. But whatever our financial status, there are monetary principles we should understand and apply if we are to protect our families. And now, *when you are first married* (or even before), is the time to lay hold of these fundamental concepts.

Settle the Financial Issues First!

Jesus warned that "You cannot serve both God and Money" (Matthew 6:24, NIV). In our materialistic society, the desire to acquire more and still more—either money or possessions—can quickly lead a couple into financial trouble. One of the first warning signs is a reliance on credit.

Making a purchase on credit is not wrong, but it *is* dangerous. A recently married husband and wife move into a new apartment or house. They are happy and excited about building a life together, but there is so much that they "need"—a new refrigerator, dishwasher, bedroom set, and second car. They don't like the idea of arranging loans or using credit cards for these purchases, but they rationalize. "It's only temporary," they tell themselves. "We just want get our marriage started on the right foot."

The problem is that more "needs" surface the next month, and once the credit pattern has been established, it is difficult to break. The months pass and the bills keep coming. Soon the husband and wife decide it is easier to just pay the minimum monthly balance on their statements rather than pay off the entire amount. In just a year or two, the amount of debt reaches an unmanageable level.

Suppose one of you wants to build a tower. Will he not first sit down and estimate the cost to see if he has enough money to complete it?

LUKE 14:28

The couple decides to consolidate their debts into one loan. This maneuver proves to be only a temporary solution, however; overspending continues. Eventually the once-happy husband and wife, now plagued by feelings of guilt and despair, begin to argue and blame each other for their predicament. Before they know it, the words *bankruptcy* and even *divorce* enter their vocabulary.

Sadly, this scenario occurs all too frequently. According to the late Larry Burkett, former board chairman of Crown Financial Ministries, approximately 80 percent of couples seeking divorce say that the focus of their disagreements is money.

This gloomy outcome is entirely avoidable, of course. The key is for couples to talk to each other and make decisions about their spending philosophy ahead of time—preferably even before the wedding date. Credit, if it is to be employed at all, must be handled with great care. One obvious way to avoid trouble is to determine never to go into debt, and then to stick to your plan even when those "great deals" catch your eye.

Christian financial counselor and author Ron Blue puts it this way:

> The only way to get ahead financially is to deny ourselves some of the things we want. If we don't have the discipline to do that, then we will always be in debt. Remember too that unless you spend less than you earn, no amount of income will be enough.[10]

To be sure, establishing appropriate spending habits in order to get ahead financially is easier said than done. That's why I recommend that every husband and wife sit down at the beginning of their marriage to establish a family budget. An organized financial plan, taking into account likely expenditures over a period of twelve months, will go a long way toward instituting a worry-free atmosphere in your home.

Every family's priorities and preferences are unique. However, budget guides such as those offered by Crown Financial Ministries may help couples decide how much money to designate to specific areas. For instance, Crown recommends that a family with a net spendable income of forty-five thousand dollars allocate 32 percent to housing costs; 13 percent each to food and auto; 6 percent to entertainment and recreation; 5 percent each to insurance, clothing, debt, savings, and investments; 4 percent to medical and dental; and 7 percent to miscellaneous.[11] These are only guidelines, but may be a good place to start.

Another excellent way to limit unnecessary expenditures is to pay with cash whenever possible. Once you determine how much you intend to spend per month in each area, convert those amounts

Keep your lives free from the love of money and be content with what you have....

HEBREWS 13:5, NIV

from your paycheck into cash and divide them into envelopes labeled "food," "entertainment," and so on. When you go to the store or to the movies, use the money from the appropriate envelope. And when the envelope is empty, stop spending! It's a guaranteed method to establish a pattern of saving and keep you out of debt.

Many single-income couples with high spending habits, when faced with the realities of budgeting, decide that a second income is the solution to all their financial worries. Be wary of this idea. If the previously unemployed spouse takes a job, it *will* generate more income for the couple—but it also increases their ability to borrow and fall deeper into debt. When that happens, two incomes are no longer a luxury, but a necessity. Again, the best solution to overspending is not a second income, but establishing and sticking to a budget plan that works.

In all of these financial matters—deciding what to buy or not buy, establishing a family budget, determining whether both spouses will work—good communication between husband and wife is essential. Scripture designates the man as the leader in his home (Ephesians 5:23), and that applies to finances as well—yet a

The money we earn each day isn't really ours at all.

couple may find that the wife is more suited to the role of bookkeeper. Regardless of who is doing most of the spending and record-keeping, both partners should agree on their financial strategy, talk regularly about whether they are meeting their objectives, and work together to correct any problems. If you can maintain a consistent, cooperative approach to handling money, your family's financial future will be in good hands.

You Cannot Outgive God

We have spent most of this chapter discussing how to spend or save "our" money, but before we leave this subject, I must point out an important truth—the money we earn each day isn't really ours at all. Scripture says that "The earth is the LORD'S and everything in it, (Psalm 24:1, NIV) and "The silver is mine, and the gold is mine, saith the LORD of hosts" (Haggai 2:8). In other words, God owns it all.

This is why *before* deciding how much to allocate to our needs and wants we should honor the biblical principle of tithing (Leviticus 27:30) and set aside at least 10 percent of our income for God. I learned to tithe when I was a preschool lad. My grandmother would give me a dollar every now and then, and she always instructed me to place a dime of it in the church offering the next Sunday morning. I have tithed from that day to this. I also watched my father give of his limited resources, not only to the church, but also to anyone in need.

My dad was the original soft touch when someone was hungry. He was an evangelist who journeyed from place to place to hold revival meetings. Travel was expensive and we never seemed to have much more money than was absolutely necessary. One of the problems was the way churches paid ministers in those days. Pastors received a year-round salary, but evangelists were paid only when they worked. Therefore, my father's income stopped abruptly during Thanksgiving, Christmas, summer vacation, or any time he rested. Perhaps that's why we were always near the bottom of the barrel when he was at home. But that didn't stop my father from giving.

I remember Dad going off to speak at a tiny church and coming home ten days later. My mother greeted him warmly and asked how the revival had gone. He was always excited about that subject. Eventually, she would get around to asking him about the offering. Women have a way of worrying about things like that.

"How much did they pay you?" she asked.

I can still see my father's face as he smiled and looked at the floor. "Aw…" he stammered. My mother stepped back and looked into his eyes.

"Oh, I get it," she said. "You gave the money away again, didn't you?"

"Myrt," he said, "the pastor there is going through a hard time. His kids are so needy. It just broke my heart. They have holes in their shoes, and one of them is going to school without a coat. I felt I should give the entire fifty dollars to them."

My good mother looked intently at him for a moment, and then she smiled. "You know, if God told you to do that, it's okay with me."

Then a few days later the inevitable happened. The Dobsons ran completely out of money. There was no reserve to tide us over. That's when my father gathered us in the bedroom for a time of prayer. I remember that day as though it were yesterday. He prayed first.

"O Lord, You promised that if we would be faithful to You and Your people in our good times, then You would not forget us in our time of need. We have tried to be generous with what You have given us, and now we are calling on You for help."

A very impressionable ten-year-old boy named Jimmy was watching and listening very carefully that day. *What will happen?* he wondered. *Did God hear Dad's prayer?*

I saw the Lord match my dad's giving stride for stride.

The next day an unexpected check for $1,200 came for us in the mail. Honestly! That's the way it happened, not just this once but many times. I saw the Lord match my dad's giving stride for stride. No, God never made us wealthy, but my young faith grew by leaps and bounds. I learned that you *cannot* outgive God!

My father continued to give generously through his midlife

years and into his sixties. I used to worry about how he and Mom would fund their retirement years because they were able to save very little money. If Dad did get many dollars ahead, he'd give them away. I wondered how in the world they would live on the pittance paid to retired ministers by our denomination.

One day my father was lying on the bed and Mom was getting dressed. She turned to look at him and he was crying.

"What's the matter?" she asked.

"The Lord just spoke to me."

"Do you want to tell me about it?"

"He told me something about you. It was a strange experience. I was just lying here thinking about many things. I wasn't praying or even thinking about you when the Lord spoke to me and said, 'I'm going to take care of Myrtle.'"

Neither of them understood the message but simply filed it away in the catalog of imponderables. Five days later my dad had a massive heart attack, and three months after that he was gone. At sixty-six years of age, this good man whose name I share went to meet the Christ he had loved and served for all those years.

It was thrilling to witness the way God fulfilled His promise to take care of my mother. Even when she was suffering from end-stage Parkinson's disease and required constant care at an astronomical cost, God provided. The small inheritance that Dad left to his wife multiplied in the years after his departure. It was sufficient to pay for everything she needed, including marvelous and loving care. God was with her in every other way, too, tenderly cradling her in His secure arms until He took her home. In the end, my dad never came close to outgiving God.

May I urge you to give generously, not only to your church, but also to the needy people God puts in your path? There is no better way to keep material things and money in proper perspective. You can hardly become selfish or greedy when you are busily sharing what you have with others.

You see, God does not need your money. He could fund His ministries from an annual beef auction alone (He owns the cattle on a thousand hills). But you and I need to give! Those who comprehend and respond to this biblical principle will find that He is faithful to "open you the windows of heaven, and pour you out a blessing, that there shall not be room enough to receive it" (Malachi 3:10).

And don't forget the greatest blessing of all: the curly-headed, impressionable children who will one day gather around your feet, watching and listening. They will someday pass the good news on to *their* kids. That may be your greatest legacy on this earth. ❧

Bring the whole tithe into the storehouse,

that there may be food in my house.

Test me in this," says the Lord Almighty,

"and see if I will not throw open the floodgates

of heaven and pour out so much blessing

that you will not have room enough for it."

MALACHI 3:10

Guard your relationship

against erosion as though you were

defending your very lives.

The Marriage KILLERS

NUMBER OF YEARS AGO, Shirley and I took a vacation with our family and ended the trip in Washington, D.C. I had heard there was to be a special briefing on the family at the White House that day, and I decided at the last minute to attend. Because I was not on the guest list, it took me an extra ten minutes to get through White House security, and I slipped into the briefing room just before the first speaker was announced.

I recognized a friend and sat down behind her. She greeted me and said, "I don't think they've done you right."

I said, "Why not? What do you mean?"

She said, "They didn't give you enough time."

"Time?" I asked. "Time for what?"

"Why, time to speak," she said. "Didn't you know you're on the program today?"

At that moment a White House aide tapped me on the shoulder and asked if he could usher me to the platform. Apparently, the members of the staff who planned the briefing had known that I was likely to be there but had failed to tell me they were expecting me to speak! It was quite a shock to find myself looking at two hundred expectant professionals awaiting my words of wisdom.

Who knows, and who cares, what I said to those men and women that day. Whether I captured their attention is doubtful, but the White House staff certainly grabbed mine! I went from half-asleep to supercharged in four seconds. Fortunately for the audience, there were other speakers on the program that day, and one of them said some things I will never forget.

His name was Dr. Armand Nicholi, a psychiatrist at Harvard University Medical School and Massachusetts General Hospital. He spoke on the subject of parenting, especially as it relates to the mental health of children. I wish every mother and father could have heard his remarks as he quoted the latest research on the consequences of divorce and family disintegration.

Anything that interferes with the vital relationship with either parent can have everlasting consequences for the child.

DR. ARMOND NICHOLI

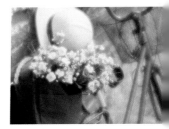

According to Dr. Nicholi, emotional development in children is directly related to the presence of a warm, nurturing, sustained, and continuous interaction with both parents. Anything that interferes with the vital relationship with either parent can have lasting consequences for the child. One landmark study revealed that 90 percent of the children from divorced homes suffered from an acute sense of shock when the separation occurred, including profound grieving and irrational fears. Fifty percent reported feeling rejected and abandoned, and indeed, half the fathers never came to see their children three years after the divorce. One-third of the boys and girls feared abandonment by the remaining parent with an intensity that researchers described as "overwhelming."

Most significantly, 37 percent of the children were even more unhappy and dissatisfied five years after the divorce than they had been at eighteen months. In other words, *time did not heal their wounds.*

In summary, Dr. Nicholi said divorce brings such intense loneliness to children that its pain is difficult to describe or even contemplate.

We all know that in the past three-plus decades divorce has become the fashionable way to deal with marital conflict. Books such as *Creative Divorce* have described it as the start of a brand-new life in the "best interest" of the entire family. But that is patently untrue. Divorce is devastating, not just for the children, but for their hurt and angry parents, too. Women pay a particularly high price, even when they are the ones who opted out of the relationship.

Let me explain. There have always been irresponsible men who were unfaithful to their wives or abandoned their families. That is still going on and accounts for millions of broken homes today. But in my lifetime, marriages have begun to disintegrate for another reason. Women, encouraged by new freedoms and financial security, have shown a greater willingness to pull the plug. I have worked with many frustrated wives who seemed determined to obtain a divorce, not because their husbands were unfaithful or irresponsible, but because romantic love was missing from the relationship. These women expressed great anger and deep resentment toward husbands who were either unwilling or unable to meet their wives' basic emotional needs.

I won't minimize the distressing "soul hunger" that women so frequently describe, but I will say this: Divorce is not the answer to it. Those who seek that "solution" are like the subject of a documentary film made during the early days of motion pictures. It shows a self-styled inventor near the top of the Eiffel Tower with a pair of homemade wings strapped to his arms. He paces back and forth, trying to work up the courage to jump. If the wings work, he'll be the first to fly. If they fail, he'll fall to his death. Finally the "flier" climbs on the rail, wobbles for a moment, then jumps—and drops like a rock.

Your love can thrive

if you give it priority

in your system of

values.

Depressed and hurting spouses who choose divorce are like that hapless man on the Eiffel Tower. They feel that they can't go back and are enticed forward by the lure of freedom—of soaring away, leaving the pain and disappointment behind them. So they jump… only to find themselves tumbling headlong into custody battles, loneliness, bitterness, and even poverty. In time, the long-term costs of their decision become clear. Some begin to see their mate's good qualities again, but by then it's too late. They've already taken the plunge.

My advice to young couples still stands: Don't permit the *possibility* of divorce to enter your thinking. Even in moments of great conflict and discouragement, divorce is no solution. It merely substitutes a new set of miseries for the ones left behind. Guard your relationship against erosion as though you were defending your very lives. Yes, you can make it together. Not only can you survive, but your love can thrive if you give it priority in your system of values.

Who knows better than the Architect of marriage that living with another person day in and day out isn't always easy? God understands what we're going through, even in our worst circumstances. Fortunately, He has given us a blueprint in Scripture for success in marriage. As Shirley and I have sought out and followed the Word of God, we have found all the stability and fulfillment in our relationship that He promised. You will, too. Marriage is His idea, after all, and His principles and values naturally produce harmony between people.

Yet it is true that the society we live in actively militates against marital stability. There are dangers on all sides, and we must defend ourselves with all our energy. Any one of these evils can rip your relationship to shreds if given a place in your lives. We have touched on some of the great marriage killers, but perhaps it would be helpful to list them and comment on a few:

1. *Overcommitment and physical exhaustion.* Beware of this danger. It is especially insidious for young couples who are trying to get started in a profession or in school. Do not try to go to college, work full-time, have a baby, manage a toddler, fix up a house, and start a business all at once. It is especially dangerous for the husband to be vastly overcommitted while the wife stays home with a preschooler. Her profound loneliness will build discontent and depression. You must reserve time for one another if you want to keep your love alive.

2. *Excessive credit and conflict over how money will be spent.* We've said it before: Pay cash for consumable items or don't buy. Don't spend more for a house or car than you can afford, leaving not enough resources for dating, short trips, baby-sitters, and so on. Allocate your funds with the wisdom of Solomon.

3. *Selfishness.* There are two kinds of people in the world: the givers and the takers. A marriage between two givers can be a beautiful thing. Friction is the order of the day, however, for a giver and a taker, and two takers can claw each other to pieces within weeks. In short, selfishness will devastate a marriage every time.

4. *Interference from in-laws.* If husbands or wives have not been fully emancipated from their parents, it is best not to live near them. Autonomy is difficult for some mothers (and fathers) to grant, and close proximity guarantees trouble.

5. *Unrealistic expectations.* Some couples come into marriage anticipating rose-covered cottages, walks down primrose lanes, and uninterrupted joy. This romantic illusion is particularly characteristic of American women who expect more from their husbands than they are capable of delivering. The consequent disappointment is an emotional trap. Bring your expectations in line with reality.

6. *Space invaders.* I am not referring to aliens from Mars. Rather, my concern is for those who violate the breathing room needed by their partners, quickly suffocating them and destroying the attraction between them. Jealousy is one way this phenomenon manifests itself. Another is low self-esteem, which leads the insecure spouse to trample the territory of the other. Love must be free and it must be confident.

7. *Alcohol or substance abuse.* These are killers, not only of marriages but of people. Avoid them like the plague.

8. *Pornography, gambling, and other addictions.* It should be obvious to everyone that the human personality is flawed. It has a tendency to get hooked on destructive behaviors, especially early in life. People think they can play with enticements such as pornography or gambling and not get hurt. In actuality, few walk away unaffected. For some, there is a weakness and a vulnerability that is not recognized until it is too late. By then they have become addicted to something that tears at the fabric of the family.

9. *Sexual frustration, loneliness, low self-esteem, and the greener grass of infidelity.* A deadly combination!

10. *Business failure.* It does bad things, to men especially. Their agitation over financial reverses sometimes sublimates to anger within the family.

11. *Business success.* It is almost as risky to succeed wildly in business as it is to fail miserably. The writer of Proverbs said, "Give me neither poverty nor riches, but give me only my daily bread" (30:8 NIV). Edward Fitzgerald said it another way: "One of the saddest pages kept by the recording angel is the record of souls that have been damned by success." It's true. Those who profit handsomely sometimes become drunk with power—and the lust for more! Wives and children are forgotten in the process.

If you are going to

beat the odds and

maintain an intimate,

long-term marriage,

you must take

the task seriously.

12. *Getting married too young.* Girls who marry between fourteen and seventeen years of age are more than twice as likely to divorce as those who marry at eighteen or nineteen years of age. Those who marry at eighteen or nineteen are one and a half times as likely to divorce as those who marry in their twenties. The pressures of adolescence and the stress of early married life do not mix well. Finish the first before taking on the second.

These are the cruel marriage killers I've seen most often. But in truth, the list is virtually limitless. All that is needed to grow the most vigorous weeds is a small crack in your sidewalk. If you are going to beat the odds and maintain an intimate, long-term marriage, you must take the task seriously. The natural order of things will carry you away from one another, not bring you together.

Let me put it another way. Not far from where I was born, the mighty Mississippi winds its way through the countryside. It is a beautiful river but has a will of its own. Approximately seventy miles from Baton Rouge, Louisiana, the government has fought a tremendous battle to keep this powerful river from changing its course to a shorter and steeper descent to the Gulf of Mexico. If the Mississippi were to have its way, the results would be catastrophic for cities and farms on the downward side. The entire topography of southern Louisiana would change. The port cities of New Orleans and Baton Rouge would lose their waterfronts and their ways of life. A town called Morgan City would be flooded into oblivion. Engineers estimate that billions of dollars of property would be destroyed if this battle were lost.

In some ways, the battle to save the family is like that. Without considerable effort and expenditure of resources, the banks will overflow and the landscape will be ruined. That's the world we live in. As we said in the first chapter, only one or two marriages in ten will generate the intimacy husbands and wives so desperately desire.

How, then, will you beat the odds and build a solid relationship that lasts until death takes you across the great divide? How will you include yourselves among that dwindling number of older couples who have garnered a lifetime of happy memories and experiences? Even after fifty or sixty years, they still look to one another for encouragement and understanding. Their children have grown up in a stable and loving environment and have no ugly scars or bitter memories to erase. Only love prevails. That is the way God intended it to be, and it is still possible for you to achieve.

But there is no time to lose. Reinforce the riverbanks. Brace up the bulwarks. Bring in the dredges and deepen the bed. Keep the powerful currents in their proper channels. Only that measure of determination will preserve the love you began with. There is little in life to compete with that priority. ❧

You who come to marriage bring

All your tenderness and cling

Steadfastly to all the ways

That have marked your wooing days.

EDGAR GUEST

I have fought a good fight,

I have finished my course,

I have kept the faith.

2 TIMOTHY 4:7

Just Passing

THROUGH

IN AUGUST 1977, my wife and children joined me on a trip to Kansas City, Missouri, for a short visit with my parents. We enjoyed several days of family togetherness before it was time to leave. As we drove to the airport, where we would say good-bye, I asked my father to pray for us. I will never forget his words. He closed with this thought:

> *And, Lord, we want to thank You for the fellowship and love that we feel for each other today. This has been such a special time for us with Jim and Shirley and their children. But heavenly Father, we are keenly aware that the joy that is ours today is a temporal pleasure. Our lives will not always be this stable and secure. Change is inevitable and it will come to us, too. We will accept it when it comes, of course, but we give You praise for the happiness and warmth that has been ours these past few days. We have had more than our share of the good things, and we thank You for Your love. Amen.*

Shortly thereafter, we hugged and said good-bye, and my family boarded the plane. A week later, my father suddenly grabbed his chest and told my mother to call the paramedics. He left us on December 4 of that year. Too soon after, my mother joined him in heaven. How quickly life changes!

Even today, so many years later, my dad's final prayer echoes in my mind. An entire philosophy is contained in that simple idea: "Thank You, God, for what we have…which we know we cannot keep." I wish every newlywed couple could capture this incredible concept. If only we realized how brief our time on this earth is, then most of the irritants and frustrations that drive us apart would seem terribly insignificant and petty. We have but one short life to live, yet we contaminate it with bickering and insults and angry words. If we fully comprehended the brevity of life, our greatest desire would be to please God and to serve one another. Instead, the illusion of permanence leads us to scrap and claw for power and demand the best for ourselves.

A very good friend of mine left his wife and children a few years ago to marry a recently divorced woman. They were both in their fifties. I remember thinking when I heard the news, *Why did you*

If we fully comprehended the brevity of life, our greatest desire would be to please God and to serve one another.

Live a life of love,

just as Christ loved us.

do it? Don't you both know that you will be standing before the Lord in the briefest moment of time? How will you explain the pain and rejection inflicted on your loved ones? What a terrible price to pay for so short an adventure!

To those of you who are young and on the threshold of married life, I hope you can bring your attitudes into harmony with this eternal perspective. Try not to care so much about every minute detail that separates you and your loved ones. It's all vanity, anyway. Solomon told us that. Have you ever tried to recall a major fight you had with a friend or a family member six months earlier? It's very difficult to remember details from even a week ago. The fiery intensity of one moment is the hazy memory of another. Hold loosely to life and keep yourself free of willful and deliberate sin. That's the key to happiness.

A Final Thought

Let me conclude with an illustration from my college days. During my freshman year, I entered the mile run in a field of about twenty men. I was in good shape and finished second to an outstanding senior who rarely lost. He graduated that year and left the vacancy to me. Unfortunately, I discovered girls in my sophomore year and I let myself get a little soft. So the next year, when it came time for the same race, I had no idea that my body was going to play dead. I walked onto the track full of expectancy and determination.

With the sound of the gun I tore off around the first turn, leaving the pack far behind. I felt marvelous. But by the second turn my side was splitting and the pack was closing in. By the time I completed the first lap, I was sucking air frantically and my chest was heaving; I must have looked like a great gray whale. Runners I had beaten the year before were passing me on every side, and I had only one desire—to get my body off the track before my lungs exploded! I collapsed on the infield grass in a sweating heap of shame and failure. I looked up just in time to see my girlfriend leave the stadium with her head down. What a tough moment for a once-proud sophomore!

Fortunately, I learned a valuable lesson that day on the track. It became clear to me that great beginnings are not as important as the way one finishes. We have all seen men and women dazzle the world and then quickly fade in dishonor and ruin. Most of life, you see, is a marathon, not a sprint. It just goes on and on, and the pressure to give up seems to increase with the passage of time.

That is certainly true in the Christian life. It is what the apostle Paul referred to when he said, "I have fought a good fight, I have finished my course, I have kept the faith" (2 Timothy 4:7). By these words, Paul was expressing satisfaction at having crossed the finish line without yielding to the pressure to cave in.

Alas, married life is a marathon, too. It is not enough to make a great start toward long-term marriage. You will need the determination to keep plugging, even when every fiber in your body longs for the infield. Only then will you make it to the end. But hang in there. Shirley and I will be waiting for you at the finish line.

Happy anniversary...the first or the fiftieth. ✽

is my prayer:

bound more and more

nd depth of insight,

y be able to discern

ay be pure and blameless

e day of Christ.

IANS 1:9-10, NIV

MARRIAGE
Resources

*E*ACH YEAR, GOD PROVIDES us with an opportunity to set aside one day to focus on our marriages; these milestone days are called anniversaries. Whether it's your first or fiftieth, let me encourage you to make this occasion truly memorable. With just a little bit of planning and imagination, you can experience a day, an evening, or a weekend you'll always remember. Admittedly, however, some of us are less gifted in the area of "creativity" than others. With that in mind, I've included a few ideas to stimulate your own thinking and planning. You'll be amazed at the dividends a brief investment of careful thought will bring to this most important human relationship in your life.

Dr. James Dobson

Ideas for Anniversary Getaways

The key word here is *memorable.* Look for opportunities to get out of the rut and routine for a couple of hours or a couple of days. A fresh setting and uncustomary activities can lift your time together out of the mundane and weave it into the stuff of memory.

1. Find a quaint bed-and-breakfast in your town or in a neighboring community.

2. Look into staying at a rustic lodge at a national park or national monument.

3. Forsake the "friendly skies" and take a train trip to another city for a night or two.

4. If you live in the country, spend a weekend in the city and enjoy the lights. If you live in the city, spend a weekend in the country and enjoy the stars!

5. Make a memory—and enjoy some laughter—by trying something neither of you has tried before: horseback riding, cruising in a riverboat or ferry, exploring a cave, going up in a hot-air balloon, riding in a dune buggy along the beach, attending a dinner theater, renting a tandem bicycle, or…?

6. Arrange a date called "Old Haunts," in which you and your spouse revisit the restaurants, theaters, or school settings that were favorites during your courtship.

Ideas for Anniversary Conversation Starters

The watchwords here are *positive, nonthreatening,* and *forward-looking.* This is an evening to enjoy! Steer away from topics that raise blood pressure, resurrect old arguments, stir up bitterness, or slog through the murk of unhappy memories. The object is to enjoy one another's company while moving your relationship in a positive, hopeful direction.

1. What two or three things would you love to see develop in our relationship in the coming year?

2. What are three major goals you would like to accomplish this year?

3. On a scale of 1 to 10 (10 being highest), where are you in your spiritual life? How might we better encourage one another in this area?

4. What are three things God has taught you over the past couple of years?

5. What friendships would we like to foster as a couple?

6. What one thing could I do more of this year to serve you?

7. What could we do to encourage another couple (spiritually, financially, emotionally) during the coming year?

8. How can we find more time to communicate, day by day, week by week?

9. Reflecting on this past year, what is the most memorable experience you've had? How about the most fun or most silly? What is the best book you've read and why?

10. Did your family have traditions as you were growing up? What was your favorite? What family traditions might we establish?

11. What new thing have you learned about me? About yourself?

12. Are you satisfied with the time commitments you've made during this past year? What would you change if you could?

13. If you could visit any five countries or cities in the whole world (and had the money to go in style!), which would they be and why?

14. What is one thing you always wished you knew how to do— and is it really too late to learn?

Don't let the enjoyment end with this celebration! Get out a calendar and schedule three special weekends together during the upcoming year; set dates and places, and discuss babysitting options if necessary.

Recommended Books

ALWAYS: INSPIRING STORIES TO ENCOURAGE YOUR MARRIAGE

by Gary Smalley and Mike Yorkey (Focus on the Family/Tyndale)

Is it really possible for a husband and wife to stay together anymore, with all of life's ups and downs?

BECOMING A COUPLE OF PROMISE

by Dr. Kevin Leman (NavPress)

Discover how to remain true to your wedding vows through the highs and lows of married life.

BOUNDARIES IN MARRIAGE

by Dr. Henry Cloud and Dr. John Townsend (Zondervan)

Only when you and your mate know and respect each other's needs can you give yourselves freely and lovingly to one another.

COMPLETE MARRIAGE AND FAMILY HOME REFERENCE GUIDE

by Dr. James Dobson (Tyndale)

America's foremost family counselor responds to nearly five hundred of the most pressing issues facing families.

DAZE OF OUR WIVES

by Dave Meurer (Bethany House)

Some marriage improvement books simply tell you to "shape up!" But here's one that will have you roaring with laughter while it strengthens your marriage.

DR. ROSBERG'S DO-IT-YOURSELF RELATIONSHIP MENDER

by Gary Rosberg (Focus on the Family/Tyndale)

Full of stirring stories and wit-coated wisdom, this book is just what the doctor ordered for increasing intimacy and reducing resentment in relationships.

GREAT EXPECTATIONS

by Toben and Joanne Heim (NavPress)

The start of a marriage can be wonderful—and a monumental adjustment. Here's great counsel for couples on building a solid foundation from the start.

GROWING A SPIRITUALLY STRONG FAMILY

by Dennis and Barbara Rainey (Multnomah)
Want a thriving faith at home—but not sure how to make it happen? Don't miss this resource.

HOW TO GET YOUR HUSBAND TO TALK TO YOU

by Nancy Cobb and Connie Grigsby (Multnomah)
They say that "women feel, and men do." This can cause big communication problems. Do you want to learn how to bridge the language gap?

THE LANGUAGE OF LOVE

by Gary Smalley and John Trent (Focus on the Family/Tyndale)
Are you often frustrated by your inability to express how you really feel? Discover how "emotional word pictures" can bring new understanding and intimacy to all your relationships.

LEARNING TO LIVE WITH THE LOVE OF YOUR LIFE

by Dr. Neil Clark Warren (Focus on the Family/Tyndale)
Discover a powerful plan for holding on to the wonder and joy of love in this insightful book.

THE LOVE LIST

by Drs. Les and Leslie Parrott (Focus on the Family/Zondervan)
Tired of all the "fluffy" ideas on revitalizing your marriage? Get intentional about revolutionizing your relationship.

LOVE MUST BE TOUGH

by Dr. James Dobson (Multnomah)
If your mate wants out, you want to know exactly what you can do to better the odds of saving your marriage. Here's the essential resource for any union in crisis, complete with do's and don'ts.

LOVING YOUR MARRIAGE ENOUGH TO PROTECT IT

by Jerry Jenkins (Moody)

Keeping marriage vows seems to be more challenging than ever for couples today. That's why it's so crucial for Christian spouses to recognize the dangers that can lead to infidelity.

THE MARRIAGE MASTERPIECE

by Al Janssen (Focus on the Family/Tyndale)

Rediscover the beauty and worth of marriage in a new light with this thoughtful, creative book.

MEN: SOME ASSEMBLY REQUIRED

by Chuck Snyder (Focus on the Family/Tyndale)

An honest, humorous look at the thought processes of men that reveals why guys are the way they are and what women can do to make the most of their mate's "quirks."

NIGHT LIGHT: A DEVOTIONAL FOR COUPLES

by Dr. James and Shirley Dobson (Multnomah)

Focus on the Family founder Dr. James Dobson and his wife, Shirley, present their first devotional for couples. It features Scripture, commentary from the Dobsons, discussion questions, and prayers.

SEX BEGINS IN THE KITCHEN

by Dr. Kevin Leman (Baker)

Find out how, by being sensitive to each other's emotional and physical needs, you can not only preserve, but improve, your marriage!

SEXUAL INTIMACY IN MARRIAGE

by William Cutrer, M.D., and Sandra Glahn (Kregel)

Most books about sex in marriage fall into one of two extremes: they're either overly "spiritual" or merely biological. Here's the best of both worlds!

SIXTY-MINUTE MARRIAGE BUILDER

by Rob Parsons (Broadman & Holman)

Got a few extra minutes to invest in your most critical relationship? Get a better marriage with this indispensable guide to lasting love.

SIMPLY ROMANTIC NIGHTS

Family Life (Marriage Activity Kit)

Feel like the flame is beginning to fade? Discover intimacy in a whole new light. Moonlit strolls. Cozy fireside chats. Candlelit dinners. And that's just the beginning…

THE SNARE: UNDERSTANDING EMOTIONAL AND SEXUAL ENTANGLEMENTS
by Lois Mowday Rabey (NavPress)
Most people don't plan to have an affair. But the truth is that such relationships don't just happen. Learn the subtle danger signs!

'TIL DEBT DO US PART
by Julie Ann Barnhill (Harvest House)
Do you have a budget, but never seem able to maintain it? Don't let financial woes create a rift between you and your spouse. Here's help.

WHAT WIVES WISH THEIR HUSBANDS KNEW ABOUT WOMEN
by Dr. James Dobson (Tyndale)
God made the sexes different for a reason. Discover the unique needs and aspirations of women that men often fail to understand.

WHEN COUPLES PRAY
by Cheri Fuller (Multnomah)
Discover a near-foolproof way to ensure marital longevity with the help of this groundbreaking resource.

*For more information about **Focus on the Family** resources, please contact:*

FOCUS ON THE FAMILY
8605 Explorer Drive
Colorado Springs, Colorado 80995
800-232-6459
or visit our website at www.family.org

Notes

1. Divorce, Provisional 1998 data, National Center for Health Statistics. http://www.cdc.gov/nchs/fastats/divorce.html (accessed 13 January 2003).

2. Walter Kirn, "Should You Stay Together for the Kids?" *Time*, 25 September 2000, 77.

3. "That's the Way I've Always Heard It Should Be" by Carly Simon and Jacob Brackman, © 1971 by Warner Brothers Music, Inc. All rights reserved.

4. William G. Axinn and Arland Thornton, "The Relationship Between Cohabitation and Divorce: Selectivity or Causal Influence?" *Demography* 29 (1992): 357–374. Larry L. Bumpass, James A. Sweet, and Andrew Cherlin, "The Role of Cohabitation in Declining Rates of Marriage," *Journal of Marriage and the Family* 53 (1991): 913–927.

5. Taken from Dr. Paul Popenoe, "Are Women Really Different?" *Family Life* 31 (February 1971).

6. Desmond Morris, *Intimate Behavior* (New York: Random House, 1971).

7. W. Cates, et al., "Estimates of the Incidence and Prevalence of Sexually Transmitted Diseases in the United States," Sex Trans Dis 1999; 26 (suppl): S2-S7, as reported in "Tracking the Hidden Epidemics 2000," Centers for Disease Control and Prevention, U.S. Department of Health and Human Services. http://www.cdc.gov/nchstp/dstd/Stats_Trends/Trends2000.pdf (accessed 17 January 2003).

8. "Sexually Transmitted Disease Surveillance, 2000," Centers for Disease Control and Prevention, U.S. Department of Health and Human Services, September 2001 (www.cdc.gov/std/stats/TOC2000.htm), as quoted in *Family News* from Dr. James Dobson newsletter, May 2002.

9. *Los Angeles Times*, 9 January 1981.

10. Ron and Judy Blue, *Money Matters for Parents and Their Kids* (Nashville, Tenn.: Thomas Nelson, 1986), 46.

11. Crown Financial Ministries, Larry Burkett's Online Budget Guide. http://crown.org/Tools/budgetguide.asp (accessed 17 January 2003).

If you desire further information regarding financial planning or budgeting, please contact:
Crown Financial Ministries
P.O. Box 100
Gainesville, Georgia 30503
770-534-1000
or visit www.crown.org